IMAGES
*of America*

THE
LAKES REGION
OF
NEW HAMPSHIRE

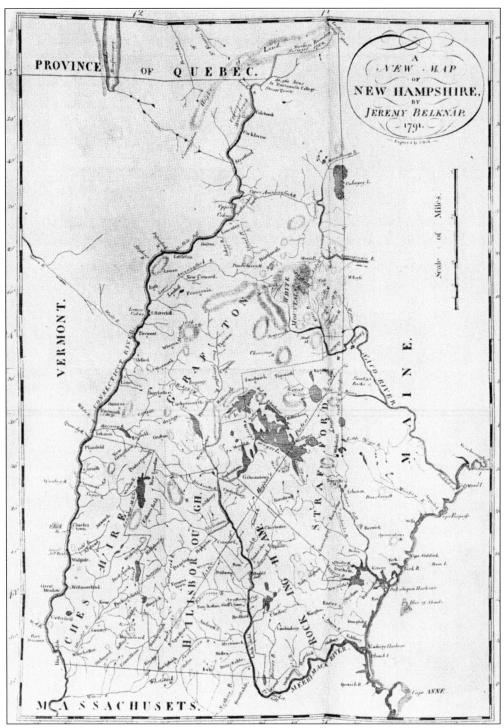

A 1796 map of New Hampshire.

IMAGES
*of America*

# THE
# LAKES REGION
## OF
# NEW HAMPSHIRE

Bruce D. Heald, Ph.D.

ARCADIA

First published 1996
Copyright © Bruce D. Heald, Ph.D., 1996

ISBN 0-7524-0455-5

Published by Arcadia Publishing,
an imprint of the Chalford Publishing Corporation
One Washington Center, Dover, New Hampshire 03820
Printed in Great Britain

Library of Congress Cataloging-in-Publication Data applied for

*To the memory of my wife, Helen*

# Contents

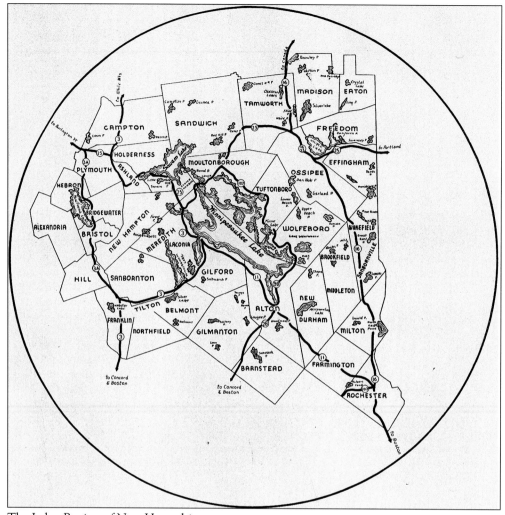

The Lakes Region of New Hampshire.

# Introduction

Beauty abounds in the Lakes Region of New Hampshire. It is easy to give a general description of the character of the shores of the many lakes, to count its many islands, and to enumerate the mountain ranges, with their names and height, that surround it. It is not easy to convey any impression in words of the peculiar loveliness that invests the region, and which lifts it above the rank of prosaic splendor.

The surroundings are scarcely less wild today then they were in 1652, when Captain Edward Johnson and Simon Willard carved their initials on Endicott Rock near Lake Winnipesaukee's outlet at Weirs Beach in Laconia. But it is not a sense of seclusion amid the forest, of being shut in by untamed hills within the heart of the wilderness, that the lakes inspire. Indeed, they are not shut in by any abrupt mountain wall. The islands and shores fringe the water with winding lines and long, low, narrow capes of green; the mountains retreat gradually back, leaving large spaces of cheerful light, vistas of gently sloping land. The whole impression is that of symmetrical beauty.

The development of New Hampshire includes many elements of history: the first settlement at the mouth of the Piscataqua and on the shores of Great Bay; the formation of the Royal Province of New Hampshire; the woeful conflict with the Native Americans and the French; the part taken by the people of the province in achieving national independence; the formation of an independent state government; the compact settlement of the state and the growth of manufacturers, railroads, and cities; and the changes in the laws, habits, and customs of the people.

Dr. Henry Vittum, Professor of English at Plymouth State College and a native of the Lakes Region, relates the following:

"You are offered here but a few glimpses of the loveliness of the Lakes Region of New Hampshire—a reflective and nostalgic history of the people, industry, and culture of its past.

Throughout the Lakes Region, breathtaking scenery and the lingering charm of bygone days captivate those who visit and also those who know the area well, and this book has tried to capture and explain some of the characteristics of a place that gives such pleasure.

This rare photographic journey through time is intended to enrich our understanding of the people of the Lakes Region, and to capture in print their legacy and their spirit for future generations to enjoy and preserve."

*The Lakes Region of New Hampshire* has been assembled with the generosity of historical societies throughout the Lakes Region, and the many friends and neighbors who wish to preserve our legacy. We affectionately recall all those memories of the bygone days, and those events and people which, over the years, have enriched our beautiful Lakes Region of New Hampshire.

Bruce D. Heald, Ph.D.

A 1909 map of Lake Winnipesaukee, created by the Boston and Maine Railroad. There are more than 1,300 ponds and lakes, 4 large river systems, and hundreds of rivers and brooks adorning New Hampshire's 9,341 square miles. All of these bodies of water have their allure, from the mighty Androscoggin to the gleaming expanse of Winnipesaukee, to the reflected beauty of little ponds like the Bear Camp in Sandwich. Nearly every mountain has its clear-watered brooks and cascades, such as Beede Falls in Sandwich Notch. Tarns that are serenity itself are frequently hidden from the highways, but are richly rewarding to the fisherman or the appreciative visitor to our Lakes Region of New Hampshire.

# One

# Lakes, Ponds, and Country Scenes

Lake Winnipiseogee and Centre Harbor Village, 1830s. Within the small bays and coves may be found the quaint little villages which make the Lakes Region so famous. It is easy to see why this area is so popular: standing atop any elevation in the region we may command a magnificent view, a vista from a God-given veranda; and from the many cottage sites, we can experience the enchantment of the wooded hillsides and rugged wilderness surrounding us.

A view of Lake Winnipiseogee from Red Hill. The lake is 504 feet above sea level, approximately 25 miles long, and between 1 and 15 miles wide at various points. The name Winnipiseogee comes from the Native American name for the lake, "The Smile of the Great Spirit."

A scene on Lake Winnipiseogee, c. 1880. The Lakes Region has been used as a recreational haven since the days of the Native Americans and the early settlers. This photograph shows the old steamer *Mount Washington* making one of its daily stops at the Center Harbor dock.

The statue of Chief Chocorua in Clough Park, Meredith Bay, Lake Winnipesaukee. There are numerous legends about the Native Americans and the early settlers of the Lakes Region. The most popular tale concerns the hunting grounds of the Winnipesaukee tribes.

As is true in all oral traditions, the tale has probably changed greatly over the years, but its essential elements are as follows: Ahanton, who was known for his warlike courage, had a daughter by the name of Ellacoya. She was a fair maiden known far and wide, but was unable to have a suitor because of her father's dislike of them. Hearing rumors of this state of affairs, a young chieftain south of the lake, by the name of Kona (the eagle), decided to test his skill and win the hand and heart of this fair maiden. Dressed in full costume, the young brave arrived at the encampment and is said to have immediately won Ellacoya's heart.

As Ahanton had traveled from the camp for a few days, the young brave was able to woo the young maiden for several days. The bliss was broken, however, upon Ahanton's return: with a sharp cry, he made an attack on the young brave for daring to woo his daughter and for knowingly taking advantage of his absence. Ellacoya, filled with great love for Kona, thrust herself between the angry men and pleaded for the life of Kona, telling her father of his display of courage when he fearlessly entered the village. Ahanton, being an admirer of courage and bravery, admitted his haste, whereupon Kona asked for the maiden's hand and was proudly granted the request by the great warrior. Many celebrations were held through the region and many feasts were enjoyed.

A few days after the wedding, a canoe party accompanied the couple halfway across the lake. It is said that while they were traveling across the mirror-like lake, a dark cloud concealed the rays of the sun, and a threatening storm began to turn the water black. Just at that moment, when the party was ready to turn back, the sun shone through, guiding the two lovers safely to the other side of the lake. "Here," cried Ahanton, "is the smile of the Great Spirit."

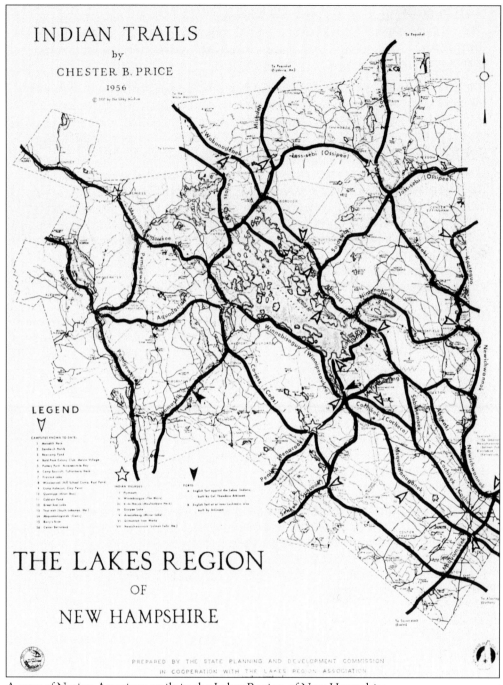

A map of Native American trails in the Lakes Region of New Hampshire.

Squam Lake. The Penacooks, a Native American tribe, referred to this lake as "Kees-ee-nunk-nip-ee," the "Goose-Lake-in-the-Highlands." Later, the white settlers shortened the name to "Kusumpy," or "Casumpa." It was also known as "Asquam," meaning "water." This latter name was shortened to "Squam."

Squam Lake, Holderness, in 1906. The waters of Squam Lake flow into the Pemigewasset River. Captain John Lovewell referred to Squam Lake in his 1724 journal: "We travelled 16 miles and camped at the north side of Cusumpy Pond." Squam Lake, with its twenty-six small islands, has long drawn summer residents. With large estates on its northern and eastern shores, it has a very conservative air about it.

A Bit of Squam Lake, N. H.

Squam Lake, Holderness. When the English settlers arrived in this area during the seventeenth century, they found life most hazardous, due primarily to the French and Indian War and the harsh climate. Persistence prevailed, and settlements were established after the Treaty of Paris and the cessation of hostilities. Five townships were then developed on the shores of Squam and Little Squam Lakes: Ashland, Center Harbor, Holderness, Moultonborough, and Sandwich.

Lake Waukewan from Beech Hill, Meredith, N. H., Lake Winnepesaukee in the distance.

Lake Waukewan from Beech Hill in Meredith in the early 1900s. Lake Waukewan was called "Wigwam Pond" for many years, but no one is sure where this name came from. Some say that the name arose after early surveyors of this area found an abandoned wigwam near the outlet in 1749, while others argue that the name was suggested by the lake's triangular, wigwam shape.

Wicwas Lake from Smith's Corner in Meredith. This lake is one of the most beautiful lakes in the township, encircled with majestic hills and dotted with wooded islands.

Chocorua Lake with Mount Chocorua in the distance, 1906. This is one of New Hampshire's most delightful bodies of water. Enclosed by tall pines, it has an air of perfect peace. Mount Chocorua is mirrored on the silver surface of the lake.

Newfound Lake—commonly known to the Native Americans as "the place where birch bark for canoes is found." This is long lake of unusual beauty lies largely in the town of Bristol. Six miles long and two-and-a-half miles wide, it is the fourth largest lake in the state. From the southern end one can enjoy an extensive view of the full length of water, with Mount Tenney at the northern end. There are four islands in the lake, the largest of which is Mayhew in the southern part.

Lake Winnisquam and Winnisquam Bridge from Winnisquam, 1911. Winnisquam means "Pleasant Water," and this 9-mile lake surrounded by low hills certainly lives up to its name. It receives its water from the Winnipesaukee River, and at the southern end sends it out to form Silver Lake, an expansion of its southern outlet which again takes the name of the Winnipesaukee River. Silver Lake, earlier known as Little Bay, was the site of Fort Atkinson, erected by provincial troops in 1746. At one time there was also a six-walled Indian fort here. Winnisquam's 25 miles of shoreline are dotted with both summer and year-round homes.

Suncook Lake and the road to Barnstead, late nineteenth century.

Ragged Mountain, located in the towns of Andover and Danbury. In the foreground is Waukeena Lake, also known as Pleasant Pond. Originally, the town of Danbury was part of Alexandria; the first settlement being made in 1771 in the southern part of the present town by Anthony Taylor, who came up the Smith River. The town was called Cockermouth until 1788, when its inhabitants asked that it be changed. It was set off and incorporated in 1795.

Squam River, Holderness, early1900s.

Wonalancet Falls, Wonalancet, early 1900s.

Whittier Falls, Ossipee Mountain Park, early 1900s.

Winter Falls on the Chocorua River. This is among New England's favorite scenes, but it is perhaps best known for its colorful reflection during the autumn season. The falls at Chocorua also present a majestic scene when cloaked in ice and snow during the cold New Hampshire winter.

A Bartlett print of Meredith in 1838.

The Center Harbor Hill road looking south to Meredith, *c.* 1905.

Red Hill, Moultonborough, in the 1830s.

Oxen breaking roads in Melvin Village, a settlement of Tuftonborough. This photograph shows local men Orlando Richardson, Ben Stokes, and John Stackpole in 1880. Although this town was granted in 1750 under the colonial government of Governor Benning Wentworth, settlement was very slow until the 1790s. On June 6, 1795, a group of early settlers sent a petition to the New Hampshire Senate and House of Representatives convening at Hanover. They testified "that we Labor under many Difficulties on many Accounts. Firstly not having no settled minister with us Nor schools which are two grate defects for the Good of Society, also on account of Rodes & many other things which might be mentioned."

They requested, therefore, to be incorporated into a township with the name of Tuftonborough. The General Court responded with typical promptness, approving the incorporation on December 17, 1795.

A Sunday afternoon ride in the Bridgewater countryside, *c.* 1880. This town is a small and pleasantly situated settlement located on the eastern shore of Newfound Lake. The center of the town was originally 4 miles east on the hill, but construction of the Mayhew Turnpike from West Plymouth to Hill in 1803 led to development around the lake shore. The turnpike was a well-used thoroughfare for traffic from the northern part of New Hampshire and Vermont to Boston. Bridgewater became known for its notable Music Colony, founded in 1932.

A view from North Main Street in Wolfeborough, *c.* 1910.

The home of Barnard H. Smith. The town line between Sanbornton and Meredith ran through the kitchen of this farmhouse.

A country scene in Freedom. Buckboards were used during the "mud season" for many years before the advent of paved roads. Both Effingham and Freedom townships embraced both the north and south sides of the Ossipee River. When granted in 1749, Effingham was known as Leavitt's Town, and the name persisted until 1778 when it was incorporated under its present name. The Wakefield and Ossipee Gores were annexed in 1820 to Effingham. Eleven years later, the territory north of the river was incorporated as North Effingham and in 1852 it assumed the name of Freedom.

The Ashland snow roller on Mill Street. Lauriston Goddard is driving the snow roller in this late-nineteenth-century photograph.

A stagecoach leaving Sandwich at the turn of the century.

# Two

# Early Village Scenes and Homesteads

Endicott Rock, The Weirs, N.H.

The Endicott Rock Monument. In 1651 the inhabitants of Strawbery Banke petitioned for a survey of the northern boundaries of the Massachusetts Bay Colony "for the establishment of a court and for the protection against the heirs of John Mason." In 1652, Captain Simon Willard and Captain Edward Johnson were appointed commissioners by the court to determine the northernmost part of the Merrimack River. They, in turn, employed John Sherman of Watertown and Jonathan Ince, a Harvard College student, to ascertain and determine the latitude of "Aquedauctan," a name given the Merrimack River where it issues out of Lake Winnipiseogee. On August 1, they found that the latitude was 45 degrees, 40 miles, and 12 seconds, besides those minutes which are to be allowed for the 3 more miles north which run into the lake. This became the southeasterly point of Meredith (Meredith Bridge), later Weirs Beach (Laconia).

The boulder remained unknown to others until 1833 when it was discovered by workmen engaged in enlarging the channel at Weirs Beach. As the markings had been worn by the elements, the state legislature appropriated money to have the rock raised and surrounded with safeguards against destruction. A facsimile of the markings on the rock was made, and it is now in the rooms of the New Hampshire Historical Society in Concord.

Wolfeboro took pride in being "the Oldest Summer Resort in America."

Main Street, Wolfeboro, 1908. The main part of Wolfeboro was granted on October 5, 1759. Five weeks later the grantees gave it the name of Wolfe-borough, honoring General James Wolfe, who had recently fallen at the Plains of Abraham, Quebec. The original grant was added to over the years. The Wolfeborough addition was made in 1800, parts of Alton were added in 1849, of Tuftonborough in 1858, and in 1895, four islands in Lake Winnipesaukee formerly belonging to Alton became part of Wolfeboro.

Replica- Governor Wentworth Mansion, Built 1769.
Wolfeboro., New Hampshire.

An artist's conception of Governor John Wentworth's summer home in Wolfeboro. In 1768 Governor John Wentworth began building an imposing summer home about 500 feet east of Lake Wentworth.

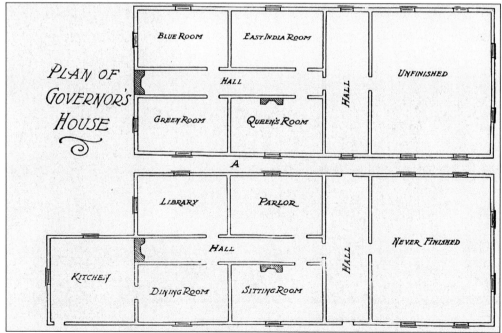

PLAN OF GOVERNOR'S HOUSE

BLUE ROOM | EAST INDIA ROOM | UNFINISHED
HALL
GREEN ROOM | QUEEN'S ROOM
HALL

A

LIBRARY | PARLOR | NEVER FINISHED
HALL
KITCHEN
DINING ROOM | SITTING ROOM
HALL

A floor plan of the Wentworth Mansion. The two-story structure was 100 feet long with a wide hall running through the first story. Everything was massive, including the windows, which were 6 feet high, and the keys to the doors, which weighed over a pound each. The mansion was never completed, though the governor took possession of it in 1770. The only remains are a restored cellar-hole and a large well.

Dan Fernald's General Store at Melvin Village, Tuftonborough, 1880s.

Boarders at Bald Peak Farm in Tuftonborough in the late 1880s.

Main Street in Center Ossipee at the turn of the century. Ossipee, incorporated in 1785, took its name from the Koos-sipe River, or from the tribe of Indians that occupied this area. The town was also known as Ossipee Gore and New Garden at different points in its development.

Main Street in Moultonboro, c. 1925. This photograph was taken looking west on Route 25 toward Red Hill. Note the Olde Country Store on the right.

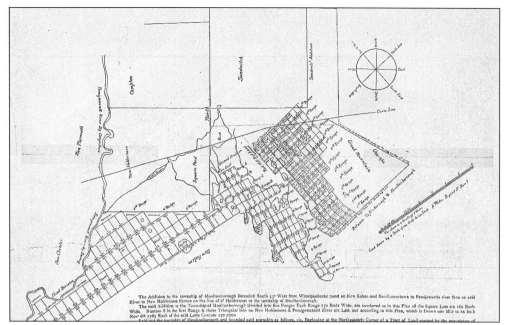

An early town map of Moultonborough. Located between the northern tip of Lake Winnipesaukee and the foothills of the White Mountains, Moultonborough was granted by the Masonian Proprietors to a group headed by Colonel Jonathan Moulton in 1763. It was incorporated in 1777.

The Olde Country Store and Post Office in Moultonborough. This establishment was first known as Freeze's Tavern, and it has been in business on the main road (Route 25) since 1793. In its various guises—as a tavern, post office, stage stop, and library—it has served the community as a social and political center for many years. In 1804, the tavern's meeting room was the site of the Morning Star Masonic Lodge.

Listed on the National Register of Historic Places, the Olde Country Store has turn-of-the-century store fixtures and houses an original Concord Coach. Its wares include cheddar cheese aged on the premises, pickles, penny candy, and other interesting items.

Lower Corner, Sandwich, c. 1900. Sandwich was a bustling town with a prosperous commercial life, the main grouping of houses being in the now somnolent Lower Corner, so-called because it lays in the lower corner of the original grant, bordering the town of Moultonborough. The old Red Brick Store can be seen on the far right.

Sandwich Village (Upper Square), c. 1900. In 1760, a party headed by Colonel Jacob Smith visited Sandwich to hunt and trap. The group discovered a small river, which they called Bearcamp, a name that has been closely associated with this region ever since. Three years later Governor Benning Wentworth granted a charter to the land to grantees (most of whom were his relatives and friends), including Nicholas Gilman and John Taylor Gilman (who later became governor). In 1770, some of the proprietors sold their rights to John Phillips. The town was named by Governor Wentworth for the fourth Earl of Sandwich, whose name is immortalized by his invention of the sandwich.

The Red Brick Store, Lower Corner, Sandwich. Before Benjamin Burley opened his store at Lower Corner in 1785, men traveled to the lake on foot, crossed it by boat, and walked to Gilmanton, where they bought their supplies and then carried them home on their backs. The second owner of the store was Daniel Little, who ran it for twenty years; and the third was Arven Blanchard, who ran it for thirty-five years, commencing in the 1840s. In recent years it has been a grocery store and T.D. Gotshall's silver jewelry shop. The retirement home of actor Claude Raines was once directly across the street from the store.

The Paul Wentworth home in Center Sandwich. Built in 1850, this beautiful Greek Revival house is presently being renovated by its present owner, Mr. Denley Emerson, who purchased it in 1952 as his permanent home on Wentworth Hill.

Tamworth Village. This small settlement was formerly known as Tamworth Iron Works. It is now popular for its quaint homes and relaxed atmosphere.

A Currier and Ives print of Center Harbor in the mid-nineteenth century. Located on the northern tip of Lake Winnipesaukee, Center Harbor has a commanding view of the lake and mountains surrounding it on the east and south. During its early years—when it was apparently known as Senter Harbor—the village was an important halfway station for stagecoaches running between Concord, NH, and Fryeburg, ME. This community was incorporated in 1797. Today Center Harbor is very popular with summer and fall visitors.

The Coe House in Center Harbor. Conspicuous on the north side of Main Street is a large white frame house surmounted by a hexagonal, multi-window tower. The house was built about 1820 by John Coe Sr., who married a daughter of Samuel Senter. A number of famous people were entertained here, including the poets John Greenleaf Whittier and Lucy Larcom, and Presidents Franklin Pierce and Grover Cleveland.

Looking south toward Meredith Center in the 1880s. The Baptist Church can be seen in the distance. This territory was first settled in 1748, and the first community was known as Palmer's Town. The name was later changed to New Salem and the community was finally incorporated under its present name in 1768. The following year Ebenezer Smith, one of the first settlers, built a log house. Later he returned to Portsmouth, bringing with him on horseback his wife, their tiny baby, and—in his pocket—a puppy.

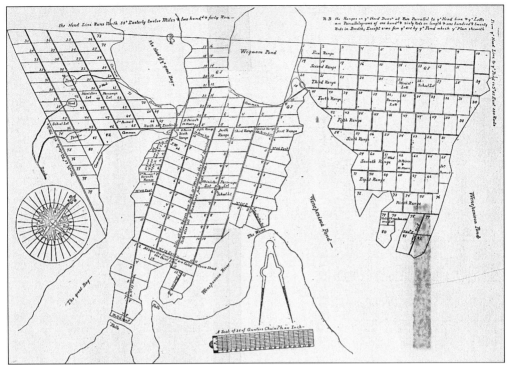

A map of Meredith. The original territory of 6 square miles was granted in 1748, but it was soon found that the indentations of the bays meant less acreage, and that a line 7 miles from the northwest corner did not reach the big bay. In 1754, the Portsmouth Proprietors increased the grant by calling the northern boundary 12 miles instead of 7; this is the present Meredith Neck. Because of dramatic events, Meredith lost a large portion of her territory to the newly formed town of Laconia on July 1855, and in 1873 also lost territory to the town of Center Harbor.

Main Street at Post Office Square in Meredith Village, *c.* 1890.

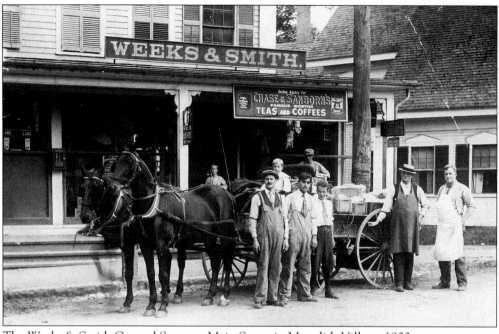

The Weeks & Smith General Store on Main Street in Meredith Village, 1900.

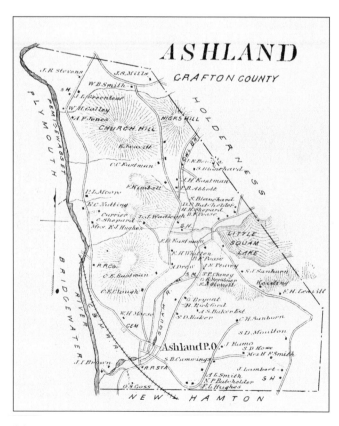

A map of Ashland.

Looking east on Main Street in Ashland in 1889. In the early days, Ashland was a part of Holderness, but it was incorporated independently in 1868. In the late eighteenth century it was home to a number of gristmills and sawmills. Today it is a thriving community; a pleasant haven for visitors to the Lakes Region.

Central Square, Plymouth, in 1890. The earliest recorded evidence of white settlers in Plymouth dates back to about 1712 when Colonel Samuel Partridge wrote from Hatfield, Massachusetts, to Governor Joseph Dudley in Boston suggesting that an expedition of approximately forty men be sent to Coassett, or Coos. Settlement of Plymouth began in 1764, and since its incorporation Plymouth has grown steadily. For many years it was a railroad junction which brought people here for trade and tourism. This community has also been the site of the present Plymouth State College for over 125 years. The original charter of the town, dated July 15, 1763, may be found in the Plymouth Town Library.

Main Street, New Hampton, in 1906. This view was taken looking southeast toward the village church. In 1763 General Jonathan Moulton of Hampton, one of the original grantees of this general section, presented Governor Benning Wentworth with a 1,400-pound ox. He shrewdly refused any payment except a small gore of land—which proved to be over 10,000 acres—adjoining the town of Moultonborough, of which he was already a proprietor. At its incorporation in 1777, the general requested that the new town be named for Hampton, his native town.

Central Square, Bristol, in 1890. Bristol, granted in 1753 as a part of New Chester (later Hill), was set off and incorporated in 1819. It was named for Bristol, England. At first a farming community, it was spurred to commercial activity—including the woodworking and woolen industries—by the opening of a railroad from Franklin in 1848.

Central Street, Franklin Falls, in 1890. This community is typical of small New England industrial cities. Situated at a junction of the turbulent Pemigewasset River and the mildly flowing Winnipesaukee River where they meet to form the Merrimack, Franklin's mills and factories had an abundance of water power.

Before the colonial first settlement, this part of the township of Salisbury was the headquarters of the Abenaki tribe. The founder of Pemigewasset (East Village), which later became Franklin, was Ebenezer Eastman, who built a sawmill here in 1764. Eastman kept a tavern here as well as running his farm and a lumber business.

Looking south on Main Street in Franklin in the 1920s. Franklin's history parallels that of Salisbury, since it was part of that town until 1828, when it was incorporated as the town of Franklin, taking its name from Benjamin Franklin. Sanbornton, Northfield, and Boscawen also contributed portions of their township to the new town. It was granted a city charter in 1895.

Tilton, N.H., The Island and Winnepesaukee River.

Tilton Island in Tilton, c. early 1900s. Tilton was originally part of Sanbornton, and the first settlement of that town occurred within the limits of what is now Tilton in 1765–66. The attempt to form Tilton was made nearly a century later, with a petition presented to the General Court of the State of New Hampshire in 1850. In 1860, the Town of Sanbornton held two special meetings to consider the matter, but nothing was accomplished until nearly a decade later. The act incorporating the town of Tilton was finally approved on June 30, 1869.

ELM ST., GILMANTON IRON WORKS, N.H.

Elm Street in Gilmanton Iron Works at the turn of the century.

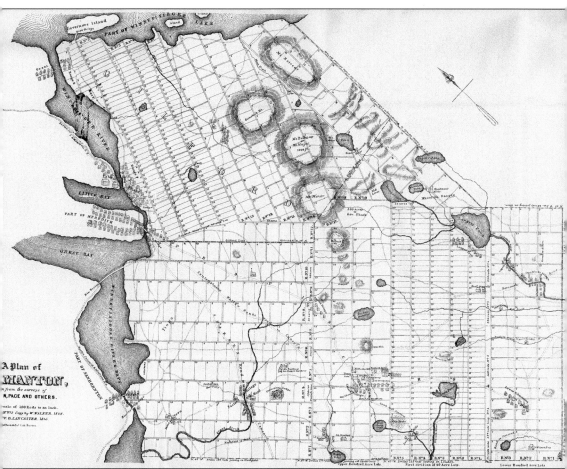

An early town map of Gilmanton. Gilman Town was incorporated by 177 people in 1727. Twenty-four of them were named Gilman—hence the name Gilman Town. The name was later shortened to Gilmanton. Its original territory included parts of the present Gilford, Laconia, and Belmont. Factories using local iron were erected as early as 1768, but were abandoned in just a few years. The present community was incorporated in 1859.

The Old Store, Gilmanton, 1880s. The first general store was opened in the 1790s by Benjamin Weeks in his home. As the population increased, other stores were opened.

Looking south on Main Street in Belmont. Originally part of Gilmanton, this area changed its name to Upper Gilmanton in 1859, and to Belmont ten years later. Until 1859, the name Gilmanton applied to the present towns of Gilmanton and Belmont; prior to 1812 it also applied to Gilford.

The old store and hall in Belmont. This building, which was built by George Riley in 1874 and later owned by Haven Grant and Fred Hall, stood near the monument at the north end of Main Street. It was torn down in 1927. The South Church can be seen at the rear along with Alvin Bean's meat cart.

John Morrison's Post Office and General Store in Winnisquam. Lake Winnisquam and the bridge crossing the lake towards Laconia can be seen in back of the store.

Gilford Village and Mount Belknap in the late nineteenth century. The first settlement of this area is said to have taken place in 1777, the year James Ames and Captain Samuel F. Gilman took up land in the "Upper Parish," the northern part of Gilmanton. On June 5, 1811, the inhabitants of the "Upper Parish" presented a petition to the General Court of the State of New Hampshire in order to form their own township. On June 16, 1812, the New Hampshire Senate passed the bill separating the "Upper Parish" from Gilmanton.

Kimball's Castle, Gilford, in 1906. In 1897 Benjamin Kimball of Concord, president of the Boston-Montreal Railroad and the Kimball and Wright Wheel Mfg. Co., hired an architect to build a castle overlooking Lake Winnipesaukee on Locke's Hill in Gilford. The castle is built of top stones that were quarried in Concord and brought to Laconia by train. From here the stones, together with fieldstone and granite taken from the vicinity of Locke's Hill, were transported up the hill by teams of horses and oxen. The Italian masons employed to build the castle boarded on Kimball's steamer *Lady of the Lake* which was docked in Glendale. The steamer was disposed of upon completion of the castle.

Bank Square, Laconia, in 1914. Laconia was originally known as Meredith Bridge, but after the annual town meeting on March 13, 1855, this section of town separated from Meredith in July of that year, and formed the new town of Laconia. Laconia remained a town until 1893, when it received its city charter. The Honorable Charles A. Busiel, who later became governor of New Hampshire, was the city's first mayor.

Union Avenue in Lakeport in 1920. Over the years there have been many names applied to this section of Laconia. In many instances the settlement was spoken of as the Upper Village, this name arising from its position above Meredith Bridge on the Winnipesaukee River. It was also known as "Batchelder's Mills," "Furnace" Village, "Slab City," and "Folsom's Falls." However, "Lake Village" was used fairly constantly, and this was the general name that continued through various forms such as "Lake City" and "Lakeville" to the name used today, "Lakeport."

Centre Barnstead in the 1890s. This town was granted to the Reverend Joseph Adams (the uncle of President John Adams) and others of Newington in 1727; settlement began in 1768. Among the early settlers was Colonel Richard Sinclair, whose wife was known for bringing hay 30 miles from Newington on a hand sled. Barnstead profited from the building of the Province Road in 1770.

Alton Bay in the 1880s. Alton Bay, located at the lower end of Lake Winnipesaukee, is a perfect port for all lake vessels. This photograph shows the *Mount Washington* at dock near the meeting ground.

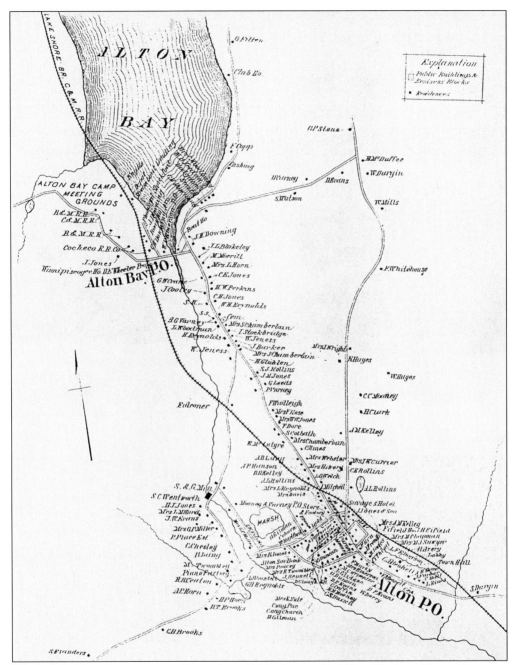

Alton and Alton Bay in a map dating from 1892. Once called New Durham Gore, Alton was settled in 1770. When it was incorporated in 1796, the citizens requested that it be called Roxbury, but Governor Wentworth gave it the name of Alton after a town in England. At one time small factories flourished here, but very few such operations are still in existence.

48

# *Three*
# Early Industries

A saw mill at Centre Harbour, with Lake Kamasatka to the left and Red Hill in background, c. 1830. Today the area shown in this W.H. Bartlett steel engraving would be Route 25 looking northeast.

A traveling merchant in Sandwich in the 1880s.

Logging at Livermore Falls in Holderness. This spot is most admired by the angler, for trout and some of the most beautiful specimens of land-locked salmon can be caught at these falls. The State Fish Hatching establishment was located here for these reasons. Logging was a major industry in the area, but sawmills also dotted the shores of most waterways throughout the Lakes Region.

The Old Mill on Beach Brook, east of Tuftonboro.

The Boody Gristmill on the Melvin River, Melvin Village, 1830s.

The old blacksmith shop in Belmont. This business was located on Main Street, near the location of Penny's Market. When the store building was moved here, the blacksmith shop was moved to the rear, where it was used for many years before it finally burned in the early 1920s.

The blacksmith shop at Gilmanton Iron Works, c. 1907. From the smithy's forge came a long list of items: hinges, tableware, ox shoes, and nails—many items that the early farmers could not make themselves. It is not surprising that the first trade to be established in Gilmanton was blacksmithing. According to early records, the first smith to arrive was Samuel Blaisdell in 1789. He settled in the Lily Pond area, which is now part of Gilford.

A saw and gristmill, Upper (Fellows) Dam, Belmont. This mill was built after a previous structure was washed out in the freshet of 1852. In 1872, shingle-making machinery was added and from 1876 until the structure burned in May 1885, it was used for the manufacture of cases for the hosiery mill.

A mill at Weeds Mills in Sandwich.

Ice harvesting at Pout Pond, Belmont, 1905.

The gristmill on Cow Island (Guernsey Island). Guernsey Island was settled in 1812 by Paul Pillsbury. Pillsbury erected a gristmill there, and is said to have been the founder of the now famous Pillsbury Flour firm. The first herd of Guernsey cattle imported to America was brought to this island to graze, which accounts for the island's name. The man on the front steps is Leon Shepherd.

The Meredith Shook and Lumber Company. Located on Lake Winnipesaukee, this company was a major employer in Meredith for many years. The company gathered raw lumber from the local countryside, took it to the shore of the lake, and from there used powerful lumber steamers to tow it to Meredith Village. The manufacturing company was located where Saint Charles Catholic Church now stands.

The Cole Manufacturing Company in Lake City (Lakeport). The Honorable Benjamin J. Cole was the head of this company for nearly half a century, having bought, in 1836, the foundry established here by his father in 1827. He developed an extensive business, including a large iron-and-wood machine shop, the buildings for which were erected in 1852. In 1872 the concern was incorporated, and a year later a steam forge was added and the manufacture of car axles commenced. The operation produced hosiery needles, bobbin and sawmill machinery, and all kinds of forgings, castings, and iron works.

The Pemmigewasset Power Co. in Franklin. Over the years, a number of mills were started in the Lakes Region, and by 1828 the use of water power in the industry had become an established fact. Sawmills and gristmills were followed by paper mills, knitting mills, and factories for making machinery, tools, and textile needles.

Laconia and the Lake Village Water Works in 1908. The water works were located at the outlet of Lake Winnipissiogee in Lake Village (Lakeport).

A mill on the Winnipesaukee River in Franklin. The first planing mill in this section of the country was located in Franklin, but it was destroyed by a freshet in 1824. Another planing mill, built by the Morrisons, burned about 1850, and in 1855 the costly structure known as the Granite Mill, built in 1822, met with a similar fate. The erection of the Franklin Mills in 1863 proved a great benefit to the village. The Upper Dam at Franklin Falls was built about 1852 to create power for a two-story hosiery mill erected at the same time. This mill was built of stone but it was also destroyed by fire.

The J.W. Busiel & Co Hosiery Mills. "Constructed in 1823, the Belknap Mill is the oldest unaltered brick textile mill in the United States. Once a hosiery mill, it houses an intact hydraulic power plant and a bell cast by George Holbrook, apprentice to Paul Revere. The Busiel Mill, built in 1853 as a hosiery mill, was later used for the manufacture of clocks, electronic relays and organs" (Belknap Mill Society, Laconia, NH).

The Sam Hodgson Hosiery Mill. This mill was in business from 1876 to 1889. In 1877, Mr. Hodgson began manufacturing stockings in the Meredith Mill. He erected new buildings, and by 1885 the mill employed approximately 160 operators, most of whom were women. The mill was located where the Mill Falls Inn and Market Place is now.

M.T. Stevens & Sons, the proprietors of Franklin Mills at Franklin Falls. The mechanical facilities here included 15 sets of cards and 120 broad looms. Employment was afforded to 250 hands, and, as the demand for ladies dress goods increased, the annual output reached higher figures. M.T. Stevens & Sons' fabrics were handled by the leading dealers throughout the entire United States in the nineteenth century.

Gilmanton Hosiery Mills, a division of the Ipswich Manufacturing Co. Employees of the Gilmanton Hosiery Mill in Belmont are shown here during the 1880s. The one-story addition to the original structure can be seen at the left, but the dormer windows had not yet been removed, nor the flat roof installed. Note the number of young employees.

Squam Lake Woolen Co. Mills, Ashland, in the 1880s. The first woolen mill in Holderness Village, now Ashland, was owned by Joseph Shephard. There were two woolen mills in the town during the 1840s, the Ashland Woolen Mill and the Squam Lake Woolen Mill. Mr. James F. Briggs, a native of Leeds, England, built the Squam Lake Woolen Mill in 1840. It operated for eight years and then became idle until September 1, 1881, when it was leased. It then changed hands several times. In 1896, Mr. Briggs sold the mill to Robert A. Hart, of Lowell, Massachusetts. Heavy coating materials and broadcloths were manufactured. The mill consisted of buildings on the east side of the river.

The Ashland Knitting Company. This company, formed in 1886, was originally composed of Thomas P. Cheney, George E. Scribner, N.P. Batchelder, and Hiram Hodgdon. They purchased the Baker mill and water privileges, and erected a three-story building measuring 110-by-54 feet. There were seven sets of cards. The mill produced more than 12,000 ladies' hose per day and employed three hundred people. Many of the employees worked at home.

A woolen mill in Bristol in the early 1900s.

Arthur Page in his blacksmith shop in Tamworth, *c.* 1930.

The late Arthur Corliss of Tamworth making baskets of split ash, *c.* 1940.

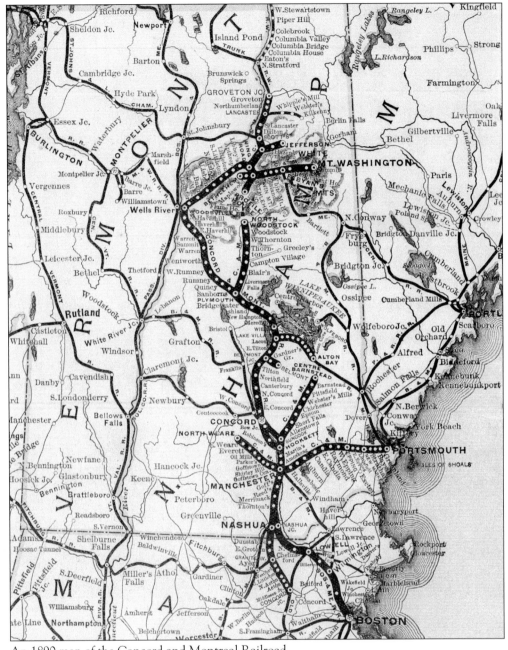

An 1890 map of the Concord and Montreal Railroad.

# *Four*
# Railroads, Steamboats, and Ports

The first train to arrive in Wolfeboro. On August 19, 1872, the first train was pulled in by Eastern Railroad No. 66, a woodburner built by Hinkley & Williams in 1871, shown here at Wolfeboro Falls. A little more than a century and a half ago, there was not a mile of railroad track in New Hampshire; no "iron horse" had invaded its valleys or passes. It was still the day of the stagecoach, which seemed to many to represent the limit of speed in transportation. A New Hampshire newspaper asked, "What can be more palpably absurd and ridiculous than the prospects held out of locomotives going twice as fast as stagecoaches?"

On June 27, 1835, the Concord Railroad Corporation obtained a charter for a railroad between Nashua and Concord. On August 8, 1848, the Boston, Concord, and Montreal Railroad established a road between Concord and Meredith Bridge—an important development in the growth of the region.

Wolfeboro Railroad Locomotive
No. 250 hard at work on the Bonhomie
& Hattiesburg Southern in 1940.

The Brookfield Station. This station, located two miles from Sanbornville, was a flagstop. It is shown here in the 1930s, in a decaying condition.

The Wolfeboro Railroad Station in 1875. Note the Eastern Railroad train and two coaches loading up before making the journey to the hotels and to Melvin Village.

The Sanbornville Roundhouse about 1880. This stall roundhouse and machine shop burned in 1911, and was replaced by a three-stall building. Sanbornton is a small settlement in the town of Wakefield. Wakefield Township was granted by the Masonic Proprietors in 1749 to John Horne and others, but was called Hornstown and later Easttown. At its incorporation in 1774 it received the present name of Wakefield.

The Wolfeboro Dock Station in 1880. At one time, this dock was a junction for three different railroads. This photograph shows an Eastern Railroad train connecting with the Boston and Maine Railroad steamer *Mount Washington*, with the Boston, Concord, and Montreal Railroad steamboat *Lady of the Lake* docked at the pier in the foreground. The large Boston and Maine building in the background burned in 1899.

The railroad station and post office, Center Ossipee, in the late nineteenth century. White's General Store can also be seen.

The Franklin Falls Depot, Franklin, in 1910. Originally this station was located off the Boston and Maine Railroad, on a spur line from Concord to Bristol. From this depot another line went directly to Lebanon and White River Junction where it connected with the Central Vermont Railroad and the Valley Railroad which ran up the Connecticut River Valley into Canada.

The arrival of the first train on the Belmont and Tilton spur line, August 17, 1889.

Main Street, Tilton, in 1908. The railroad depot can be seen on the left. The village of Tilton was located on the Concord and Montreal Railroad line, 18 miles north of Concord, 93 miles from Boston, and 10 miles from Laconia. This rail connection, and the stage connections with the adjacent town of Franklin on the Northern Railroad line, made Tilton a very active commercial center for the region.

The railroad depot in Veterans Square, Laconia, in the 1930s. When the Boston, Concord, and Montreal Railroad was extended to Meredith Bridge, the passengers were provided with a small wooden station, which soon became inadequate as the community grew. After the merge of the Boston, Concord, and Montreal Railroad and the Concord Railroad to form the Concord and Montreal Railroad in 1889, the new railroad company immediately proceeded to modernize its many railroad stations. Charles A. Busiel, a prominent Laconia businessman, and one of the railroads managing directors, made sure that a new station was built in his city. The city responded to this effort by widening Depot Street in order to create the present Veterans Square to serve the heavy traffic and make this an appropriate entry to the city. On August 22, 1892, the station was dedicated and opened to the public.

The Weirs Beach Railroad Station, *c.* 1880s. The Weirs was a popular resort on the western shores of Lake Winnipesaukee and the chief port on its shores reached by the railroad and the major steamers. It is the scene of much activity during the summer, particularly when seasonal boating is in full swing. The Weirs is the starting point for the *Mount Washington.*

The Weirs Beach Railroad Station in 1907. The Weirs derived its name from a Native American fishing weir located near Endicott Rock. The Native American village Aquadoctan was located on the hills to the north and west, and it was the largest such village in this region. The ruins of the weirs, a triangular enclosure of rocks and logs used for trapping fish, could at one time be seen in the waters just north of Endicott Rock.

The Boston and Maine Railroad Station, Meredith, in the early 1900s. When the railroad came to Meredith in 1848, it changed the complexion of the town for years to come. Over the rails came the coal that would power local steam engines, such as the one at the Meredith Linen Mills. Approaching the tracks along South Main Street, the freight depot was on the left and the passenger station (shown above) on the right.

The Winona Railroad Station sometime before 1925. This was a very popular stop for travelers between 1880 and 1920.

The Ashland Railroad Station. The Boston, Concord, and Montreal Railroad ran the first train from Concord to Plymouth on Friday, January 18, 1850. The regular passenger service started on Monday, January 22, with one train daily from Concord. This was due at Ashland about 11:45 am and left Ashland on the return journey to Concord about 12:30 pm. Many people will remember the long canopy at the Ashland station which provided shelter during bad weather.

Rail service through Plymouth with the Pemigewasset Hotel in the background. This station is located 126 miles from Boston. The station is a little above the Pemigewasset River, while the village is situated upon a terrace reached by a sharp grade from the railway station.

An electric trolley car at Weirs Beach. This was a popular means of transportation between Laconia, Lake Village, and the Weirs during the early part of this century.

STEAMER "LADY OF THE LAKE."
Connecting Wier's Landing. Boston. Concord, & Montreal R.R., with Wolfboro' and Centre Harbor, N.H.

The *Lady of the Lake*. This vessel was built by the Winnipesaukee Steamboat Company and launched at Lakeport in June 1849. She was the first lake passenger steamer and she operated in this capacity until 1893, when she was finally retired and sunk in Glendale Bay.

The steamer *Stella-Marion* on Newfound Lake in Hebron. Hebron, a small hamlet at the upper end of the lake, was incorporated in 1792 from parts of Plymouth and Cockermouth.

The sidewheeler *Mount Washington* approaching Weirs Dock in 1929. In 1872, the Boston and Maine Railroad Company launched this fine sidewheeler at Alton Bay. She was considered the most beautiful sidewheeler ever built in the United States. A single piston, with a diameter of 42 inches and a stroke of 10 feet, drove this vessel at more than 20 miles per hour. The horsepower was 450 at full ahead, more than enough to leave any of her competition in her wake.

The Steamer *Governor Endicott* at Melvin Village Landing in 1910. In 1905, the Winnipesaukee Transportation Company commissioned Irving M. Cottrell to construct a new vessel, and the *Governor Endicott* was launched during the spring of that year at Lakeport. The vessel was 100 feet long with a beam of 19 feet. The new boat was placed in general service, supplementing *Belle of the Isles* on the Melvin run and doing an extensive excursion business. The first captain of this new boat was Leander Lavallee.

*Uncle Sam* at the Bear Island Dock and Post Office in the 1930s. The third mail boat was the original *Uncle Sam*, built in 1906 for Mr. Seabury of Long Island, New York. The single screw vessel was 65 feet long, had a 14-foot beam, drew 7 feet of water, and was capable of carrying 100 passengers. In 1945, this boat was converted from the traditional steam to the new diesel-type engine and she kept her franchise on the lake until 1961, when she was retired. The mail service continues today via the *Sophie C*.

Captain Edward Lavallee delivers the daily mail at the Bear Island Post Office, 1970.

The *Mount Washington*, 1880s.

The *Mount Washington* and the *Cyclone* at Weirs Dock in the 1880s.

The *Sophie C.* at the Meredith Dock in the mid-1940s. In 1969, the mail franchise was placed with the *Sophie C.* This vessel was built by the General Ship and Engine Works of East Boston, Massachusetts, and launched at Center Harbor in August 1945, for the sole purpose of being a shuttle service between Wolfeborough and the Weirs. The vessel, like her predecessors, services the many islands in the northern end of Lake Winnipesaukee. She is presently owned by the Winnipesaukee Flagship Corporation of Weirs Beach.

A boat landing at the Weirs in the early 1900s.

A boat landing at Wolfeborough in the early 1900s.

A boat landing at Alton Bay in the early 1900s.

The *Mount Washington* leaving Weirs Dock, *c.* 1880s. Governor's Island can be seen in the background. On December 22, 1939, this fine old vessel burned at Weirs Dock, ending a legacy of sixty-seven proud years of sailing on beautiful Lake Winnipesaukee.

## *Five*
# Hotels and Taverns

Life at the grand hotels in the Lakes Region of New Hampshire was carefree in the late nineteenth century.

The Oak Birch Inn at Alton Bay, 1900.

The Central House in Holderness, c. 1880. The present Squam Lakes Science Center used to be a hotel. It was known first as the Central House and then as the Holderness Inn. The most elegant hotels in the Holderness area were the Asquam House (which crowned Shepard Hill until it was torn down in 1946) and the Towers (also known as the Mount Livermore House). Located on Livermore Cove, the Mount Livermore House burned in a spectacular fire in 1923. It is still possible to see a stone with the name of Jewell, the proprietor, carved on it.

The Asquam House in Holderness. Located on a promontory between Squam Lake and Little Squam Lake, Holderness is a thriving summer resort with the feel of an English village. The original town grant of 6 square miles on the Pemigewasset River was made by Governor Benning Wentworth in 1751. The following year lots were laid out in the rich intervale beside the Squam River. In 1761, Governor Wentworth issued a grant for the township, naming it New Holderness for the Earl of Holderness. The grantees were Major John Wentworth and sixty-seven other Episcopalians. Originally devoted to agriculture and lumbering, its situation on Squam Lake and easy accessibility began to draw visitors to it after 1870.

The Ballard House on Parade Road in Meredith, *c.* 1907.

The Elm Hotel on Main Street in Meredith Village, 1920. Many travelers who visited the Lakes Region village inns testified: "Host and hostesses sit at the table with you, and do the honors of a comfortable meal. Upon going away, you pay your fare without haggling. You meet with neatness, dignity and decency. The chambers neat, the beds good, the sheets clean, supper passable, cider, tea, punch and all, total for fourteen pence a head."

An advertisement for the Long Island House read: "The house—with cottage—when comfortably filled accommodates 50 people. It is on a rise of land 70 feet above the level of the lake, is 50 rods from the steamboat landing, and from the house and grounds can be had magnificent views of the lake and islands. It is supplied with milk, poultry, vegetables, etc., from the farm and has a well-stocked ice-house. Each department is in charge of some member of the family, and great care is taken to give as far as possible the comforts of home. Terms, from $7.00 to $12.00 per week, according to room, number occupying the same, and length of stay."

Lakeside House in the Weirs, 1900.

Pemigewasset House in Plymouth in 1915. The first structure of this fine hotel was built about 1863 by John E. Lyon, president of the Boston, Concord, and Montreal Railroad. When it burned, the railroad rebuilt it, and made it accessible from the station by a flight of stairs. Nathaniel Hawthorne often stopped here, and here he died (in room no. 9) on May 18, 1864. In 1909, the Pemigewasset House burned again, and a new hotel was rebuilt on Highland Street where the present Lamson Library now stands.

The Alton Bay Inn as it appeared in the 1930s.

The Colonial Hotel in Centre Harbor. This hotel was originally known as the Senter Hotel. Its promotional brochure boasted that there were two covered verandas, one on the lake side and another facing the hills and mountains. The office, main dining, and serving rooms were on the first floor, and in addition to these were a nurse's and children's dining room and drawing, music, ladies, writing, reading, and smoking rooms. The hotel was supplied with pure Mountain Spring Water from the famous "Belknap Spring." There were fifteen double fireplaces and ninety-one sleeping rooms. The name of the hotel was later changed to The Colonial. On June 20, 1919, the grand old hotel was destroyed by fire.

The dedication ceremonies of the Kona Fountain, 1907. This photograph shows the Reverend William P. White, the Countess of Frankenstein and Mrs. Herbert Dumaresq (her daughter), Dr. Leonard B. Morrill, Mr. Herbert Dumaresq, Ms. Margaret B. Slade, Reverend John Thorp, and Mr. Orville P. Smith standing on the platform addressing the townspeople of Centre Harbor. The Colonial Hotel can be seen in the background.

Hotel Elmwood in Wolfeboro.

The Bear Island House on Bear Island in Meredith. This hotel was started as a boarding house by Mr. and Mrs. Leonard Davis in 1879. According to *Bear Island Reflections*, published by the Bear Island Conservation Association in 1989, "The guests at Bear Island House enjoyed hiking, tennis, swimming and boating. Behind the hotel were clay tennis courts and bath houses. It was customary for boarders to stay for weeks at the hotel, which required a large staff to work in the vegetable garden, milk the cows, gather the eggs, roll the tennis courts, run the boats, and, of course, clean rooms and wait on tables." The hotel closed in October 1934, and in November of that same year fire destroyed the fine old establishment.

The Tavern Hotel in Laconia, built in 1913 on the corner of Church and Main Streets. For years this fine hotel hosted many dignitaries, including Dwight D. Eisenhower during his presidential campaign in 1953. The landmark operated as a hotel until the late 1960s, and at one time was considered "The newest and most modern fireproof hotel in NH; service unsurpassed. Long distance telephone in every room. Rooms with bath. Hot and cold running water in every room." Since 1970 the hotel building has been used as housing for the elderly.

The Garnet Inn and Annex, Center Harbor, in the 1930s. An advertisement for the inn read as follows: "A modern all year-round hotel at the base of Garnet Hill near the shore of Lake Winnipesaukee, a wonderful view of Lake Winnipesaukee is obtained from the hotel piazza." This hotel was extremely successful during the early 1900s and among its visitors were the Roosevelts and the Duponts. Next to the Garnet Inn was a large building known as Independence Hall (later Lamprey Hall). In 1922, the old building was purchased and rebuilt by Mr. Bennett, who called his acquisition the Garnet Inn Annex and used it as twenty-two more guests rooms.

DIAMOND ISLAND HOUSE IN 1861

Diamond Island House with the *Lady of the Lake* at dockside in 1861. This hotel was moved across the ice on Lake Winnipesaukee during the winter to become a part of the Old Hotel Weirs, which later burned on November 8, 1924.

New Hotel Weirs, Lake Winnipesaukee, N. H.

The New Hotel Weirs. This elegant hotel overlooking Weirs Bay was said to be the best hotel in the Lakes Region. It had 250 rooms and 50 bathrooms and was open from May to October. In 1907 rates were $2 and $2.50 a day and $10 and up per week. Unfortunately, this grand hotel and a dozen other buildings were destroyed in the worst disaster ever to befall the Weirs; it burned on November 8, 1924.

Lake Winnipesaukee From Hotel Weirs, N. H.

A view from the Hotel Weirs, with the railroad station and the *Mount Washington*.

The dining room at the Hotel Weirs in 1885.

## HOTEL ✳ WEIRS,

Weirs, Lake Winnipesaukee, N. H.

D. B. STORY,                    Proprietor

### Monday, August 3, 1885.

## DINNER.

—SOUPS.—

Turkey Soup.

—FISH.—

Baked Sword Fish, Hollandaise Sauce.
Cucumbers.

—BOILED.—

Fowls with Pork.

Corned Beef with Cabbage.          Leg South Down Mutton, Caper Sauce

—ROAST.—

Beef, Dish and Brown Gravy.

Lamb, Mint Sauce.                  Spring Chicken, Giblet Sauce.
Veal, Stuffed, Brown Gravy.

—COLD MEATS.—

Roast Beef.          Corned Beef.          Ham.

—ENTREES.—

Macaroni with Cheese.
Boiled Carolina Rice.              Queen Fritters with Maple Syrup

—VEGETABLES.—

Round Potatoes.                    Shelled Beans.
Mashed Potatoes.      Cabbage.     Boiled Bermuda Onions.
Cucumbers.                         Green Peas.
Sliced Tomatoes.          String Beans.          Beets

—PASTRY.—

Danish Pudding.

Apple Pie.            Coconut Pie.            Blueberry Pie.
Lily Cake.       Chocolate Cake.      Fruit Cake.
Jelly Rolls.          Sponge Cake.
White Bread.          Graham Bread.          Brown Bread

—DESSERT.—

Lemon Ice Cream.                   Coffee Ice Cream.

Watermelon.
Oranges.          Castanas.          English Walnuts.
Pecans.          Almonds.          Filberts.
Layer Raisins.                     Crackers and Cheese
TEA.                               COFFEE.

Waiters are provided with wine cards and list.

An 1885 menu from the Hotel Weirs.

89

The old Gilmanton Tavern. Noble houses lined both sides of the Old Province Road when it was laid out in 1770. In 1793 the Gilmanton Tavern was built at the crossroads, almost directly behind the unique signboard with its five arms stretched in three directions. Today, the old tavern stands elegantly on Route 107 in Gilmanton Corners.

The Winnecoette at the Weirs in 1883. This building later became known as the Brickyard Mountain Inn. An advertisement for the hotel read as follows: "The view of the lake, mountains and islands from its grounds and piazzas offers a picture of natural scenery unsurpassed in New England, and makes this spot well worthy of its Indian name."

The Lane Tavern in Sanbornton. The original tavern was built *c*. 1810. Its ownership in the early decades is not clear, but we do know that it was kept by Mr. Chase Jaques in 1826. Also, it is certain that J. Hilliard Lane was the innkeeper from 1836 to 1844. This tavern occupied an important spot on a main stagecoach line between Concord and the North Country. It was used for local gatherings as well as being a busy hostel until about 1840, when the railroad came through Tilton, altering life, and especially travel, in this region. The Town of Sanbornton was incorporated in 1770.

The present Lane Tavern in Sanbornton.

The Farrar Tavern. This tavern was built in 1782 beyond the Shad Path on the Parade Road in Meredith Bridge. The earliest record to it is a reference in a deed from Ebenezer Smith to his brother, Jeremiah Smith, which includes a note that reads: "... bounded on the north by land which I this day deeded to Mary Farrar."

# Six

# Schools and Landmarks

The old schoolhouse, as drawn by J. Warren Thyng. The system of education in New Hampshire developed from the methods established by the first settlers. From these early colonial days, our state has taken the leadership in providing its youth with the best possible education.

New Hampton School in 1906. This private school, located in the center of the village and housed in a row of red brick buildings of the American Georgian type, was founded in 1821 by William B. Kelley and Nathaniel Norris. Shortly after 1825, the charter of the school was amended and the school became the New Hampton Academical and Theological Institute under the control of the Baptist denomination. In 1853, a new charter was granted to the New Hampton Literary and Biblical Institution with control transferred to the Free-Will Baptists.

The school building in Lewiston, Maine. In 1870, the theological department was moved from the school to Lewiston, Maine, and since then the establishment has been a college preparatory school. Among its many graduates have been nine state governors, several college presidents, a justice of the supreme court, and a number of prominent editors. This school is considered one of the finest in secondary education in all of New England.

The Holderness School. This privately endowed educational institution is located on a high terrace overlooking the Pemigewasset River.

The central building is a fine example of Southern Colonial style. Two gabled-end wings admirably balance the main structure. The small brick dormitory is notable for its steep sloping roof which gives an unusual effect on the exterior, and additional space on the interior. This secondary school is ranked high in the academic community, and attracts many students from all over the country.

Gilmanton Academy, founded in 1794. On June 20, 1794, a charter was obtained for an academy. In 1796 the first academy building was erected, at the Center Village, Gilmanton Corner, on land donated by the Honorable Joseph Badger Jr. This was the fourth academy in the state at the time. On January 22, 1808, the academy building was entirely consumed by fire, and on February 24, just four weeks and four days after the fire, the frame of the second academy building was erected. For ninety years the academy was the focal center of the community. Like a mighty heart its living principles pervaded the community. This was considered to be the grandest monument the fathers of Gilmanton ever built.

The Brewster Free Academy, c. 1920. Brewster Academy occupies a 40-acre site running from Main Street in Wolfeborough to the shores of Lake Winnipesaukee. In the center of the grounds stands the academy. Built in 1905 to replace an earlier structure, it is a large, two-story, hip-roof building built of brick, with a dignified entrance sheltered by a pedimented portico with paired Ionic columns. This main building contains the administrative and academic classrooms of the school. The academy offers a four-year college preparatory course and secondary education to "any person deserving to attend and receive instruction."

Tilton Seminary, c. 1906. This school, which was established in 1845 under the sponsorship of the Methodist Episcopal Church, was incorporated in 1852 as the New Hampshire Conference Seminary. In 1923, the present name, Tilton School, was adopted. The school has a general and college preparatory program, offering individualized instruction. Today, we rank this private school among the finest in the nation.

The old Smith Meetinghouse in Gilmanton Center. This church bore the first footprints of Christianity in the town. It was erected in 1774 near the center of the town of Gilmanton, overlooking a wide territory. Near it was the residence of Reverend Isaac Smith, the first pastor. The first courthouse, the first burying ground, and the first public school were also established in this area. In 1840, owing to the organization of the churches at the Academy Village and the Iron Works, the old edifice was taken down, and the present Smith Meetinghouse was erected, largely with material taken from the first building.

The New Hampshire State Normal School, Plymouth. This building, Rounds Hall, was dedicated on August 28, 1891.

For 125 years, this educational institution has been responsible for guiding, inspiring, and motivating young adults to excel. Located in central New Hampshire, at the foothills of the White Mountains, this college has progressed from a "Normal School" for training teachers to that of a highly accredited college of many disciplines under the name Plymouth State College of the University System of New Hampshire.

The Chapman School (Middle Road, schoolhouse No. 9), Tuftonborough, in 1906. This photograph shows, from left to right: (front row) Bernice Hersey, Lillian Hoyt, Irving Hoyt, Carroll Lamprey, and Raymond Stitt; (back row) Lottie Adjutant, Fred Hoyt, Harold Stitt, Ben Ferguson, Harry Doe, Walter Pringle, Roscoe Adjutant, Gladys Adjutant, Angie Hersey, and Louise Pringle. The teacher, Miss Ethel Horne, is not included in this picture.

The Ashland Grammar School in Ashland. The Ashland Graded School, as it was called, was built in 1878. Three departments were established—Primary, Intermediate, and Higher Grammar—and all were housed in four rooms. Due to large enrollments in the early 1900s, two rooms were made on the top floor and kindergarten was abolished, leaving grades one through nine. Students desiring further education at that time were given the choice of attending Plymouth, Tilton, or New Hampton schools with tuition paid by the town, but with transportation costs paid by the family. Today, these facilities house children from kindergarten through grade eight; grades nine through twelve attend Plymouth Regional High School.

The Meredith Village Schoolhouse on Main Street. Located high on a hill in the village, the schoolhouse was the center of local education until it was replaced in 1914 by the larger brick building which became known as the Meredith High School, and later the Humiston Building.

DUDLEY LEAVITT
1772-1851

Author and publisher of almanacs first appearing in 1797. Best known was "Leavitt's Farmers' Almanac and Miscellaneous Year Book" which was continued after his death for about 45 years. This publication provided information vital to domestic and agricultural life of the period. He lived in house 200 yards east.

The Dudley Leavitt historic marker is located on Route 25 East, at the Meredith-Center Harbor town line, approximately 100 yards south of his homestead.

Dudley Leavitt. During the early days of education, one name stands before all as the predominant teacher in New Hampshire: "Master" Dudley Leavitt (1772–1871). So influential was his teaching that scholars from hundreds of miles away traveled to the Lakes Region to be taught by him. Not only did he teach in our public schools, but he also taught privately in his home, established the Meredith Academic Academy, and wrote several published texts. This teacher's accomplishments as an educator and citizen of distinction gave much to the moral fiber of our local citizens.

Ordination Rock and Monument in Tamworth. This monument indicated the site of the First Meetinghouse, built in 1794. The rock is a large flat-topped boulder now surmounted by a small marble obelisk. On this rock, on September 12, 1792, the Reverend Samuel Hidden was ordained as pastor of the church organized on that date. For forty-six years he was the guiding light of the settlement.

Devil's Den in the Gulf, Sanbornton, in 1912. Just to the right on Interstate 93 are rock formations called the "Gulf." A description from Farmer and Moore's *Gazetteer of New Hampshire* reads as follows: "Extending nearly a mile through very hard, rocky ground some thirty-eight feet in depth, the walls from eighty to one hundred feet asunder, and the side so nearly corresponding as to favor an opinion that they were once united."

The Concord Coach. This original coach is presently the property of the Sandwich Historical Society, and it is generally used for the Sandwich Fair Parade which is held in early October each year.

Durgin Bridge No. 45 in Sandwich. Originally built in 1828, the present structure is the fifth over the easily flooded Cold River. This bridge was named for James Holmes Durgin (1815–1873) who operated a gristmill near this crossing, drove the stagecoach from Sandwich to Farmington, and was a link in the Underground Railroad. This bridge is one of the few remaining wooden Paddleford truss bridges in New Hampshire. It has an overall length of 110 feet and an outside width of 19 feet. The roadway within the bridge is 96 feet long and 14 feet wide. It was built by Jacob Berry.

The Whittier Covered Bridge in the 1880s. This bridge was named for the poet John Greenleaf Whittier, who summered in this community. Here he wrote *Among the Hills, The Voyage of the Jettie, Sunset on the Bear Camp,* and other famous works. Half a mile south of West Ossipee is a row of fine maples, the most southerly of which are known as the Whittier Maples, as Whittier apparently worked under them. This bridge crosses the Bear Camp River.

Daniel Webster's birthplace in Franklin. This small, two-room frame house, located off Route 127, is the spot where the famous statesman and attorney spent his boyhood years. Built about 1780, it was restored in 1913.

The Plymouth courthouse in which Daniel Webster made his first plea. This building is situated on Court Street diagonally across from Plymouth State College's Rounds Hall.

The Gale Memorial Library and the Soldiers Monument, on the corner of Church and Main Streets in Laconia. The monument to the left was "Erected by Laconia In Honor Of The Heroic Valor And Patriotic Service Of Her Sons During The Civil War. To Our Country's Defenders." On the right is the Gale Memorial Library, an attractive stone structure dating from 1898. On the second floor of this library is a very fine museum exhibiting the history of the Lakes Region.

THE ARCH
TILTON N.H.

Tilton Arch. The name of the new town was adopted in honor of the Tilton family, which had been very prominently identified with the settlement and development of Sanbornton since Deacon Nathaniel Tilton settled there between 1768 and 1771. The family name is also commemorated by the Tilton Memorial Arch, a unique structure built of hewn stone with height of 55 feet and a width of 40 feet. Between the columns of the arch is a device of polished Scotch granite bearing up a Numidian lion. On this device is the inscription "Tilton, 1883," and each end of the keystone bears the legend "Memorial Arch of Tilton, 1882," in raised letters.

The dedication of the Civil War Monument (Soldiers' Monument) on Highland Street, Ashland, on May 30, 1899. Ashland contributed eighty-three men to the Union during the Civil War. The monument is of Concord granite with bronze tablets on four sides. On three sides are the names of all the soldiers from Ashland. The monument is 4 feet square, and the column is 11 feet high and 2 feet in diameter. The whole is surmounted by a 7-foot bronze statue of a soldier at parade rest. In 1900, the town voted to move a drinking fountain, at the junction of Main, Thompson, and Mill Streets, to make way for the monument. St. Mark's Church can be seen on the far right.

The Boy Scout Memorial on the Common in Plymouth.

The Chocorua Island Chapel on Squam Lake in 1910.

The Grave by the Lake memorial in the Melvin Village Churchyard. This particular marker was immortalized by John Greenleaf Whittier in his poem by that title.

The Crow's Nest at Ossipee Mountain Park in Moultonboro. Mr. Shaw built a lookout seat with an overhanging roof on a spot where the castle now stands, and Ossipee Mountain Park was opened to the public.

"Castle in the Clouds." The "Castle Springs" is located on the brow of the Ossipee Mountain Range, overlooking Lake Winnipesaukee. This exquisite stone house was the home of Thomas Gustave Plant, who called it "Lucknow" and lived there from 1913 until his death in 1941.

The Kona (Dumaresq) Fountain in Centre Harbor. On September 23, 1907, Mr. Herbert Dumaresq, in a notable act of generosity, gave a beautiful drinking fountain to the village of Centre Harbor. This fountain has been a source of pride for the community. The granite block from which the fountain sculpture was cut was reputed to weigh 10 tons. The sculpture was done by Samuel Russell Gerry Crook of Lincoln, Massachusetts, a nationally known ceramic artist and sculptor and a protege of Augustus Saint-Gaudens, one of America's most famous sculptors.

The Spindle Point Light House. In 1892 Colonel Charles H. Cummings built this stone tower, located at the most southern extremity of Spindle Point on Observation Road in Meredith Neck. The tower stands 50 feet high and has a 12-foot diameter at its base. Today, it serves as a beacon for navigators and tourists alike.

Becky's Garden. This is the smallest chartered island in Lake Winnipesaukee. It is located at the northern tip of the lake near Center Harbor. The house was built by Lewis P. Kelly of Centre Harbor specifically for this island.

## Seven
# Potpourri of Nostalgia

John Greenleaf Whittier, in the doorway of the Sturtevant farm in Center Harbor in 1885.

A parade of oxen at an early Sandwich Fair.

Anxious passengers await the sidewheeler *Mount Washington* to dock at the Center Harbor Town Dock. In the background, the Colonial Hotel stands majestically overlooking Lake Winnipesaukee.

President Theodore Roosevelt addressing veterans of the Grand Army of the Republic in Veterans Grove on August 28, 1902. This is presently the site of the New Hampshire Veterans Association Headquarters at the Weirs.

The Encampment Headquarters at the Weirs in 1908.

The campgrounds at Alton Bay in 1906. The Second Advent Campmeeting held its first meeting on September 7, 1863, overlooking Lake Winnipesaukee at Alton Bay. This land was leased from the Boston and Maine Railroad and later purchased. The first participants lived in tents.

The Alton Bay Campmeeting Association was incorporated in 1876. Over the years, a large tabernacle, a central kitchen, and a bakery were built. On August 23, 1945, the fear of fire was realized. About noon, an oil stove exploded and fire spread rapidly. Twelve fire companies responded and pumped water from the lake, and by evening the fire was under control. No one was injured or killed, but three chapels, the tabernacle, the seated grove, the bookstore, and 260 cabins were destroyed. The campground continued to grow, however, and also to prosper, with summer camp meetings, conferences, and retreats for young people.

A house on Mission Circle at the campgrounds in 1906.

A moment of reflection under the old oak on Meredith Bay in 1915.

An old chaise in the 1913 Plymouth Pageant Parade.

Camp Sandy Island. This vacation camp for young adults and families has been operated by the Boston YMCA for many years. It is credited as being the first educational adult camp in the country.

The Mess Hall at Camp Idlewild, Cow Island, Tuftonborough, in the 1920s. This camp was first settled in 1892. For many years it was operated by the L.D. Roys family, until it closed in the 1970s.

An early steamboat docked near the shore at Green's Basin in Moultonboro.

Mrs. Milton (Eve) Seeley and her Chinook Kennels sled dog team in Wonalancet. During the 1930s, many of the dogs in both the Wonalancet and the Chinook Kennels were trained for dog-sled races that were a main feature of winter carnivals held throughout New Hampshire and Canada in winter months. At these kennels were a large variety of Siberian huskies, Alaskan malamutes, Eskimos, and Chinooks, which were bred and trained by Mr. and Mrs. Milton Seeley.

The 60-meter ski jump at Belknap Mountains Recreation Area in Gilford. In 1937 the first international ski contest was held on this ski jump.

A country auction at Sandwich in the 1930s.

A pulling contest at the Sandwich Fair.

A small girl with some Guernsey calves at Steele Hill Farm in Sanbornton.

Pausing at the spring in Melvin Village in 1901. This hamlet was selected by Thomas Dreier and writers of his ilk as a permanent retreat amid scenery and serenity. The beauty of this community is unsurpassed with the massive Ossipee Mountains as a background and the waters of Tuftonborough Bay in the foreground. Numerous summer cottages line the waterfront.

Nothing's too big to handle for this young man at the Sandwich Fair!

A 1936 flood scene on the Pemigewasset River in Plymouth.

The steamer *Mount Washington* at the Weirs. Note the period costumes and the type of luggage being boarded for an afternoon excursion. The captain at this time was Leander Lavallee.

Launching the M.V. *Mount Washington II* at Lakeport in 1940. This boat replaced the old *Mount Washington*, which was destroyed by fire in 1939.

The *Uncle Sam II*. In 1962, the *Uncle Sam II* made her appearance on the lake, after a laborious overland journey from the Portsmouth Naval Shipyard. This vessel was a converted PT boat. On March 23, 1963, under the dual ownership of Vernon Cotton and Allan Perley, she slipped through the water on her maiden voyage to serve the many islands in Lake Winnipesaukee. Postmaster Ed Lavallee prepared the mail and luggage on board, thus giving the boat the continuing distinction of being a floating post office.

There is a lot of wildlife on the islands. The animals also come down to the dock to meet Captain Wilbur Bigelow during his daily mail delivery from the *Sophie C*!

Meredith's Town Crier greeting the *Mount Washington* at the Meredith Dock on July 31, 1968, as part of the Bicentennial celebrations.

A glimpse of Newfound Lake in Alexandria. This lake is one of the larger lakes in New Hampshire. It is approximately 6 miles long and 2.5 miles wide. Alexandria, like other towns in the area, was part of the Masonian grant of New Chester, and was not incorporated until 1782.

Sailing on Lake Wentworth in Wolfeboro in the 1930s. This beautiful lake is 4 miles long and 3 miles wide. It was formerly known as Smith's Pond. Smith's River (which connects Lake Wentworth with Lake Winnipesaukee) and Smith's Bridge (the part of Wolfeboro situated near the outlet of Smith's River) derive their names from the same source—an English hunter by the name of Smith who visited this region. The lake is somewhat oval in shape and covers an area of 3,094 acres. It has twenty islands, the most important of which are situated in the central part of the lake.

The Sanbornton town snow roller being led by eight horses in 1918.

Ice boats on Paugus Bay in the 1940s.

Parading on the boardwalk at Weirs Beach in the 1940s.

Irwin's Winnipesaukee Gardens Ball Room at the Weirs in the 1930s. For many years, this popular dance hall was where people from all over New England came to dance to the music of the most famous "Big Bands" in the country.

Three Mile Island. The first permanent camp of the Appalachian Mountain Club was established at Three Mile Island in 1900. The island, made up of some 43 acres, is located at the northern end of the "Upper Broad" in Lake Winnipesaukee. Half a mile long and less than a quarter of a mile wide, the island is practically a ledge, rising to a height of about 50 feet in a ridge running north and south in the center of the island. Pictured above is the island's dock and recreation center as seen in 1942.

Jolly Island Dock on Lake Winnipesaukee in the 1930s. Local inhabitants patiently await the arrival of their daily mail from the *Uncle Sam*. Here the island family enjoys the beauty and solitude of their surroundings.

The end of a long day's work. John Flanders is in the buggy and Charlie Robinson is standing by the horse.

# Acknowledgments

Special thanks are extended to the following individuals, towns, and historical societies for their contributions to this volume: the Andover Historical Society; Alton and Alton Bay, NH; Ashland, NH; Barnstead, NH; Mildred Beach, Belmont, NH; Robert and Barbara Bennett; the Bear Island Conservation Association; Glades J. Bickford; Hector L. Bolduc; the Boston, Concord, and Montreal Railroad; D. Warren Boyer; Bridgewater, NH; Bristol, NH; Lewis R. Brown; Catherine H. Campbell; the Center Harbor Historical Society; Chocorua, NH; Barbara Cogswell; Franklin, NH; the Gilford Historical Society; the Gilmanton Historical Society; *Granite State Monthly*; Gilbert M. Hewins; Steven Holden; Holderness, NH; Barbara Kelley; the Laconia Historical Society; the Lakes Region Association; Charles S. Lane; Beth Lavertue; Robert Lawton and *THE WEIRS TIMES & Tourists' Gazette*; Richard F. Leavitt; The Meredith Historical Society; the *Meredith News*; the Moultonboro Historical Society; *New Hampshire Troubadour*; New Hampton, NH; Ossipee, NH; William Pond; the Plymouth Historical Society; Chester B. Price; Walt Reyelt; James H. Rollins; David Ruell; the Sanbornton Historical Society; the Sandwich Historical Society; Tamworth, NH; Tilton, NH; the Tuftonboro Historical Society; Rudy VanVeghten; Henry Vittum; Jean and Charles Whitten; Dorothy Wilkins; and the Wolfeboro Historical Society.